This Book Belongs To:

Window to My World

ISBN: 978-0-578-56800-3

WINDOW TO MY WORLD

By **Tré Cavil**

Illustrated by **Anastasia Yatsunenko**

Window to My World

When your parents are always on you
to make sure that you're polite,
reminded daily of your actions wrong and right.
When your sibling is being selfish
and all they do is cause a fight,
all you want is to hide from out of sight.

Like your smile makes others happy,
you have the ability to create.
Your actions change your day from bad to great.
So, take this invitation
and make sure that you're not late
and leave your worries and your troubles at the gate.

This magic place is full of wonder
with an entrance white and pearled.
Every smile you see is extra wide and curled.
Come bring your imagination
for this place is twist and twirled,
and welcome to the Window to My World.

Open Me

Open me if you're looking for grins.
Go on and come in, come in!
Or if you just want to look and see,
go ahead and open me.
Open me if you're looking for laughter,
a good morning after,
or just want a reason to smile.
Open me and please come in,
and won't you stay for a while?

Recycle

Recycle this.
Recycle that.
Recycle your neighbor's cat.
Recycle plastics, cans, and tins.
Recycle paper plates and pens.
Recycle good.
Recycle bad.
Recycle your mom and dad.
Take their hands and walk them in
and turn them into kids again.

Man on the Moon

Someone tell the man on the moon
to please pick up a sweeping broom.
For the white and glowing spot
has got some dingy dirty spots.
The entire moon is turning gray,
so when you see him, will you say,
"Please pick up your sweeping broom,
kindly sir, and clean it soon."

Lost and Found

Lost and found!
Lost and found!
Somebody lost, and then I found,
right here lying on the ground.
What was lost, now is found.
So, if you detect that something's lost,
come and pay the ten-cent cost,
and I'll show you what I've found
in my lost and found.

Polka Dot Parrot

I have a polka dot parrot
who will never eat a carrot
but eats his spinach and peas.
No matter if I scare it,
or even if I dare it
to eat one with crackers and cheese.

Grandfather Clock

My grandfather is stuck
in the tall skinny clock.
I say, "Hello Gramps,"
and he *ticks* and he *tocks*.
From morning to evening,
he's right on the dime.
On every one hour,
he gives a big chime.
My grandma is funny
for the things that she'll say,
but grandpa just tells me
the time of the day.
Sometimes as I pass,
I'll stop and say, "Hi!"
but *tick* and then *tock*
is his only reply.

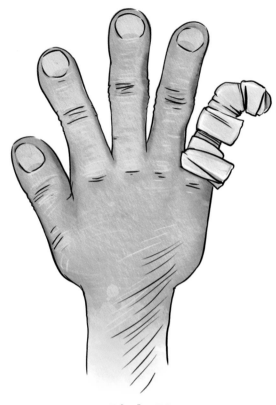

Pink-E?

The thumb is the fattest one,

it mainly does the chore.

The pointing one?

I don't know what that one's really for.

The middle is surrounded, so it's never left alone.

The ring finger usually has jewelry around its bone.

The little one?

I know I'll never really understand:

Pinkie or pink-E?

It all depends upon the hand.

Tickle Me

Tickle me this.
Tickle me that.
Tickle that big alley cat.
If he licks you and rubs your leg,
then you're okay.
But if he swipes you while he hisses,
you better run and pray he misses!
And hopefully you can get away
to tickle him another day.

Dog Catcher

My name is Dick Fletcher.
I'm the town's dog catcher,
and you know what I've come to believe?
I don't need a net or a trap to be set.
I just need an arm and a sleeve.

Monster in My Bed

I have a giant monster
that sleeps beneath my bed,
but when he's having nightmares
he sleeps with me instead.

Lucky Rabbit's Foot

I had a lucky rabbit's foot,
or should I say a rabbit?
I only wanted the rabbit's foot,
but he wouldn't let me have it.
I offered money and asked polite
but all he said was, "No."
So, I tied a string around his leg
and went everywhere he'd go.
Sometimes he skipped.
Sometimes he hopped.
Sometimes I had to duck.
But then one day,
the string came loose,
and I ran out of luck.
Somehow, he tied the string to me,
and the knot won't come undid.
So, instead of being my lucky rabbit,
I'm his lucky kid.

How Many?

How many ticks are in a clock?
It would take too long to count them.
How many rides are in a horse?
I'm just too scared to mount them.
How many bites are in a steak?
Depends how big you bite it.
How many years are in a bike?
Depends how well you ride it.

Tic-Tac-Toe

Tic-Tac-Toe,
three in a row—
that's the name of the game.
But what if you have three in a row,
and none of the shapes are the same?

Benny Badback

Benny Badback has a bad back.
When he walks, his back is bent.
Benny Badback has a bad back,
and he dropped his twenty cents.
Benny's bad back *cricks* and it *cracks*
when his spine is fully bent.
Benny's bad back will not bend back—
but he got his twenty cents!

Proper Pig

I'm the most Porkliest,
Puggable, Pokable Pig.
I wear the most Practical,
Prettiest, Pink-colored wig.
I walk with a Primly
and Properly Pop.
That's why I'm a Pig
and not a Pork Chop.

What if the Sun Fell Asleep?

Could you ever imagine if the sun fell asleep
and didn't wake up for days?
What would we do without any light
or without any heated sunrays?
I guess we'd have to depend on the moon,
but the moon is hardly around.
It's here one day and halfway the next,
and then it's nowhere to be found.

Know a Little More

I don't know what you think,
and you don't know what I think,
but our minds will surely drink
all the lessons we adore.

I don't know what you know,
and you don't know what I know,
but if we share a little info,
we will know a little more.

The BE QUIET Man

Have you ever met the Be Quiet man?

Whatever you say,

"BE QUIET!" he says

as loud as he can.

No matter if you're polite.

"BE QUIET!" he says.

"BE QUIET! BE QUIET!"

he'll say all night.

I once said, "Hello," with a grin.

"BE QUIET!" he said. "Don't say it again!"

I said, "Hello," with a smile.

"BE QUIET! BE QUIET!" he said.

Like I haven't heard it in a while.

I once said, "Hello" in a crowd.

"BE QUIET KID!" he said out loud.

Then one day, I was fed up.

I said, "Hello, sir." He said, **"BE QUIET!"**

Then I looked at him and said, **"BE QUIET!"**

And he did.

Then I did.

Now things between us haven't been tense,

but for some reason, we haven't spoken since.

A Cow Forgotten

They used to come for milk,
but I had none to be milked.
They used to come for butter,
but I have none I used to utter.
They used to come for meat,
but I said, "It's probably rotten."
That's why I am a cow
that has sadly been forgotten.

What If?

What if red stood for go
     and green stood for stop?
What if the world turned into
     a big blue lollipop?

Can I Sleep with You?

Mommy? There's a monster in my room,
and it looked at me and growled.
I would have gone to sleep anyway,
but the monster is just too loud.
I know you hate to sleep alone,
and since your bed is made for two,
Mommy, do you think you'd mind
if I came to sleep with you?

Trapeze Artist

I used to be a trapeze artist
who did jumps with turns and flips.
I used to be a trapeze artist
who did ducks with rolls and dips.
I used to swing across the stage,
catch a book, and read a page,
double twist and spin and glide,
then triple twirl on either side.
But then one time, I forgot a dip
and fattened my bottom and upper lip.
I have two black eyes, and now you see
why a trapeze artist I used to be.

Siblings

My sister is the worst, you see.
She's always telling lies on me.
She takes my things when I don't see.
She's Grandma's favorite clearly.

My brother is one I cannot bear.
When mad, he puts things in my hair.
He's selfish, and he'll never share.
I mean these words sincerely.

We're there for each other to the end,
siblings but there's no better friend.
We sometimes fight, but then we mend,
and we love each other dearly.

Achoo!

Achoo! Achoo!
Excuse me sir—
Achoo! but I have a cold.
I've been trying to sell my cookies
but, ***Achoo!*** is the only thing sold.
People give me money, ***Achoo!*** just to get away.
I try to say, "Excuse me," but ***Achoo!*** is all I can say.
So pardon me, ***Achoo! Achoo!***
but please you have to believe,
that I didn't mean to soak your cookies
or put ***Achoo!*** on your sleeve.

Take Some

Take some happiness and joy from you.
Take some pride and excitement, too.
Take your smiles and take your grins,
take some courage, and put them in.
Mix them up real nice and slow
and give them to someone you know.

Sick Bag

In this bag
     I have a cold,
          a headache,
               and the flu,
and with them I don't know what to do.
I don't want to waste them
or throw them away,
and I don't want to save them for another day.
I wouldn't give them to a friend.
I would an enemy, but I have none.
How about you? Won't you take just one?
I'll let you pick which one you want to make you sick.
A cold,
     a headache
          or the flu?
Which one will it be for you?

Elephant Hula-Hoop

Have you seen an elephant Hula-Hoop
or ever think you will,
see an elephant Hula-Hoop
on a unicycle wheel?

Sailing the Sea

My brother, my sister,
my best friend, and me,
have built us a boat
and are sailing the sea.
To our sails and our vessel
our first mate will tend,
as the rest of us stand by
and wait for the wind.

Out to Sea

Out to sea
we went sailing.
Out to sea
we went fishing.
Out to sea
we went pailing.
Out to sea
we went swimming.
And never again
will you see us
out to sea.

Knock Knock

Knock! Knock!
"Who's there?"
"Wanna."
"Wanna who?"
"Wanna read a poem?"

Three-humped Camel

I have a camel
with two hump humps
and a one-humped camel makes two.
But if you have a camel
with hump, hump, humps,
I'll trade my two-humped camels to you.
Because my two-humped camel
is now a one-humped camel,
and my one-humped camel can't see.
I'm looking for a camel
with hump, hump, humps
because a three-humped camel rides three.

Hail to the King!

I am king!
This is my mountain,
and over there, where the birds sing,
that is my fountain.
This is my grass.
These are my trees,
and way out there are my seas.
I rule here, and when I call all my people, they'll cheer.
Hail to the king!
Hail to the king!
Then they'll join hands, and they'll sing.
Hail to the king!
Hail to the king!
I'll stand up and calm the crowd
and speak my words extremely loud.
"Anyone who's out there doubt'n.
I am the king of this mountain!"

The Reversible, Bendable, Twistable Man

The reversible, bendable, twistable man

bends and twists as much as he can.

He bends his body in eight different sections.

He twists and bends in every direction.

You Never Know

You never know what you can do

until you give a try.

So, I bent my knees, and then I jumped

and tried to reach the sky.

I grabbed around the bark today

and tried to move a tree.

I took a running start, my friend,

and tried to jump the sea.

I climbed a hill and reached up high

and tried to touch a star.

I knew it from the beginning

that the reach would be too far.

You never know what you can do

until you give a try...

"But some things are obvious, you silly little guy."

Crutches

I know I'm not the smartest guy,

but I can't get these crutches to work,

no matter how hard I try.

One is so big it's as high as the door,

and the other one doesn't even reach the floor.

I don't think that I'm doing anything wrong.

One crutch is too short, and the other is just too long!

A Seed

A seed, a seed,
I found a seed
and put it in the ground.
I'm sitting here until it grows,
so please don't make a sound.
I hope it grows into a tree,
so I can climb and play,
or for when it's really hot outside,
in its shade I'll stay.
But what if it is not a tree...
what could it possibly be?
I guess I'll have to sit here,
and I'll soon find out and see.

Have You Ever?

Have you ever been so happy
that you did nothing but smile?
Have you ever walked so far
that you swore you walked a mile?
Have you ever eaten so much
that your stomach could explode?
Have you ever been so hot
that you wish it would be cold?
Have you ever been all by yourself
and sworn you weren't alone?
Have you ever thought you'd ever read
a *have you ever* poem?

Shoehorn

I've been around
from town to town,
from cities to fields of corn.
Nowhere can I find
a man sighted or blind
to teach me to play the shoehorn.
I've knocked on doors
and two-story floors,
and nobody seems to know
what kind of sound
this shoehorn I found
makes when you know how to blow.
Does it sound like a trumpet
or a saxophone's crumpet?
I bet it sounds like a kazoo.
I'll figure it out later
when I serenade her,
but right now I can't put on my shoe.

Bungee Jump

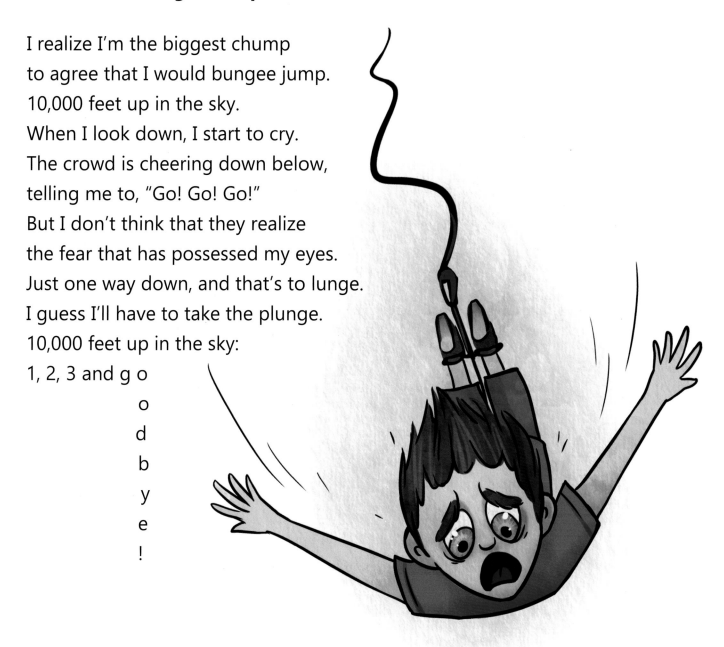

I realize I'm the biggest chump
to agree that I would bungee jump.
10,000 feet up in the sky.
When I look down, I start to cry.
The crowd is cheering down below,
telling me to, "Go! Go! Go!"
But I don't think that they realize
the fear that has possessed my eyes.
Just one way down, and that's to lunge.
I guess I'll have to take the plunge.
10,000 feet up in the sky:
1, 2, 3 and g o
        o
        d
        b
        y
        e
        !

Go!

Go team, Go team.
Rah! Rah! Rah!
Tell a joke, tell a joke.
Ha! Ha! Ha!
Win, kids. Win, kids.
Go! Go! Go!
Santa Claus, Santa Claus.
Ho! Ho! Ho!

Have You?

Have you ever seen a mouth that sniffed
or seen an eye that listened?
Have you ever seen an ear that winked
or a nose that did the kissin'?

Colorful Ape

I went to the zoo
and saw a gigantic ape
whose colors were strawberry,
lemon, and grape.
Now what would you do
if you went to the zoo
and saw such a colorful ape?

The Man With 33 Eyes

To my surprise,
I met this guy
with 33 eyes in his head.
He bumped into me in the street,
and these are the words that he said.
"Excuse me, sir, can you show me the place
that I am trying to find?
You would think I'd see in 33 ways,
but in 33 ways I am blind."
He told me about a woman he met,
the woman with 33 ears.
He said, "I'm blind in 33 ways,
and in 33 ways she can't hear."
I walked away and shook my head
I'd say about 33 times.
I couldn't figure this strange thing out
if I had 33 minds.

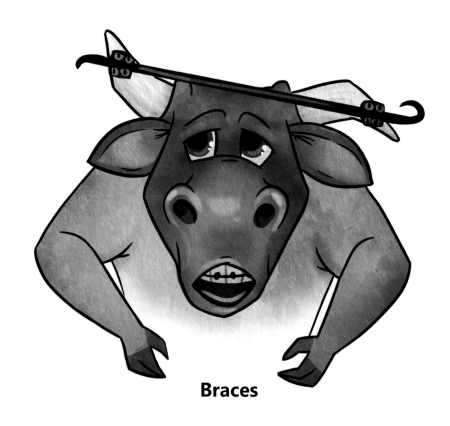

Braces

I've seen many braces
on many faces
to straighten up many teeth.
I've seen many faces
with too many braces
on top and underneath.
I've been many places
and seen many faces
since the day I was born.
But of all the faces
in all the places
I've only seen one brace on a horn.

Look in the Sky

Look in the sky! It's a bird! It's a plane!
Or is it a big yellow candy cane?
I think it's a walrus that's up in the sky,
but everyone knows that a walrus can't fly.
Oh, what can it be?
Oh, what can it be?
Is it a bush, or is it a tree?
Could it be Superman saving the day?
Perhaps it's a cherry or chocolate soufflé?
Here it comes fast and straight with a zoom.
Get out of the way!

Splish!

    Splash!

        Boom!

Oh, water balloons!

Happy Birthday

Happy Birthday!
Happy Birthday!
I'm so happy it's your birthday!
Because your birthday
is my birthday.
Happy Birthday to you and me!

Hand Stand

Some people can do a handstand.
They can even turn and twist.
I just use my hand stand
when I detach my wrists.

Trampoline

I have the biggest trampoline
that anyone has ever seen.
When I jump, I see the town.
I go way up and then come down.
I feed the birds while in the sky.
I wave at planes that pass me by.
I like to flip. I like to flop.
I'd really like if I could stop.
For my giant trampoline
has got to have the strongest spring.
So, tell my mother I said goodbye
because I think I jumped too high.

Simply Smiley

I once knew a man named Simply Smiley
who stood on a corner and waved.
Cars would stop and give him coins
and all the coins he saved.
Then one day, he took his coins
and went to cash them in.
Then Simply Smiley never had to
wave for coins again.

Messy Room

My socks, my shirt, my pants,
my hat, my shoes, my toys, and more,
are lying all together
upon my messy bedroom floor.
I've been told to clean it 20 times.
I should have listened, see.
For now, my room is such a mess
there ain't no room for me.

Rain, Rain

Rain, rain go away.
I thought I told you yesterday
to come back on another day
when I'm inside, okay?

No Rules Day

Let me see:
There's Father's Day
and Mother's Day,
Election Day
and New Year's Day,
but still there's something missing...
so I'm not quite done, okay?

There's Easter Day
and Groundhog Day,
St. Patrick's Day
and Labor Day,
but still there's something missing...
so there must be more to say.

There's Christmas Day,
Thanksgiving Day,
Memorial Day
and Veteran's Day,
but still there's something missing....
They forgot a No Rules Day!

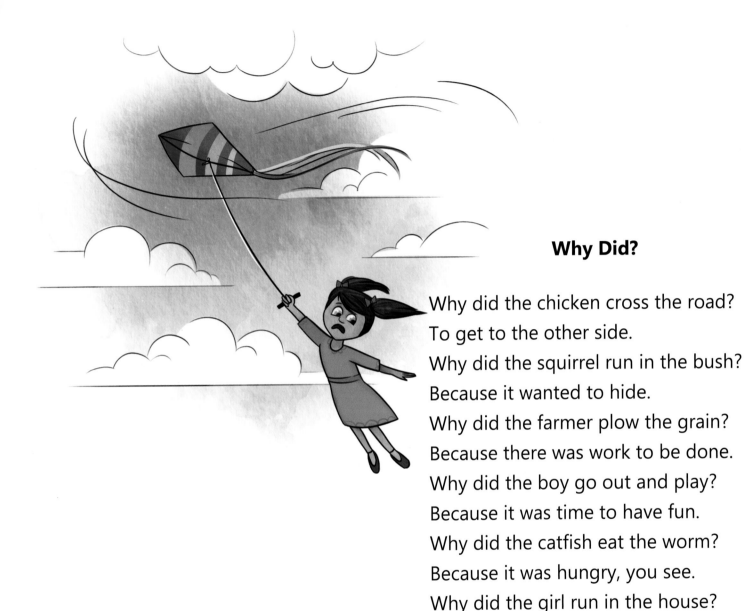

Why Did?

Why did the chicken cross the road?
To get to the other side.
Why did the squirrel run in the bush?
Because it wanted to hide.
Why did the farmer plow the grain?
Because there was work to be done.
Why did the boy go out and play?
Because it was time to have fun.
Why did the catfish eat the worm?
Because it was hungry, you see.
Why did the girl run in the house?
Because she got chased by a bee.
Why did the kite fly high in the sky?
Because it got blown by the wind.
Why do the questions have to stop?
Because we have come to the end.

Spread Your Love

Cross your fingers. Twist your knees.
Write a friend from overseas.
Help someone and do your part.
Show the world your caring heart.
Hug your friend and shake a hand.
Spread your love across the land.

Food Fight

A Pear hit an Apple right in its face,
then a pack of Grapes fought in its place.
An Orange called the police and told what he saw,
and then the police arrested them all.

Missing Teeth

Do you know of anyone
who's selling any teeth?
As you see, I'm running out
on top and underneath.
Oops! There goes another one.
I just can't keep them in.
I swear a tooth has fallen out
each time I start to grin.
And now I'm down to three, you see,
so please don't make me smile.
And add another tooth
to this ever-growing pile.

Walking Stick

"I bumped into a walking stick early yesterday."

"You bumped into a walking stick? To you what did he say?"

"Excuse me, sir."

"Then what did he do?"

"He walked off on his way."

Noah's Ark

On the lower deck of Noah's Ark:
2 pigs,
2 dogs,
2 cats.
And right beside them there they lay:
2 cows,
2 bulls,
2 bats.
On the second level of Noah's Ark:
2 squirrels,
2 snakes,
2 hares.
And right beside them there they lay:
2 elk,
2 deer,
2 bears.
And on the deck of Noah's Ark:
the wind,
the rain,
the sea.
And right among them there we stood
Noah,
you,
and me.

Freddy Friendly

I know a man named Freddy Friendly,
who is the meanest man I know.
You would think he would be more friendly
because his name says so.
But Freddy Friendly is never nice.
He's mean down to the bone.
So, stay away is my advice
because his temper's blown.

I Used to Clean

I used to do the dishes
until I broke them all.
I used to dust the vases
until I made them fall.
Now for some reason,
I don't have to clean at all.

With One

With one, the party started
then another person came.
We added up to two,
and we partied just the same.
Three more people entered,
and four were at the door.
Nine is now the answer,
but there are more in store.
The party has now doubled
and I hear a *clicky-clack*.
Four entered from the front,
and three entered from the back.
There is a couple leaving
and a person right behind.
The rest of us will party—
everything is going fine.
An hour has gone by,
and the party's half the size.
Three more girls are leaving,
and there go four more guys.
I hear someone honking.
It must be someone's ride.

The Davis twins are parting,
and one stands by my side.
But now she will be going,
and that leaves zero friends.
With one the party started,
and with one the party ends.

No Special Occasion

I know it's not your birthday
or an anniversary.
No holidays are coming,
but Mommy, can you see.
It's not a special occasion,
and I bought you nothing new.
I just want to tell you
that I LOVE YOU!

911

If you catch on fire,
stop, drop, and roll.
Don't begin to panic—
keep it in control.
If it's getting smoky,
crawl along the floor.
Before you make an exit,
make sure you feel the door.
Run and tell a neighbor
to dial 9-1-1.
Check up on your family,
and now your job is done!

Timid Tulip

I once met a timid tulip
who was shy and too timid to bloom.
It would not blossom in April or May,
and it was too timid to blossom in June.

Summer went by, and then came winter,
and spring was coming near.
I talked to the tulip and asked it please
to get over its blossoming fear.

It told me this spring it would blossom in May
if I stood there by its side,
and it would show the world the beautiful things
that it kept inside.

When spring came, the tulip blossomed with pride
with a beauty that was so unique.
Then it puckered up its delicate lips
and kissed me on the cheek.

Bananas for Sale!

Brown bananas for sale!

Brown bananas for sale!

I have brown and green bananas for sale!

Come one, come all.

They just went on sale.

Come and get your brown bananas for sale!

Out of Luck

I have a lucky sock,
a lucky shirt,
a lucky penny.
But when it comes to luck,
I have to say I don't have any.
I'm very good,
I knock on wood,
I hardly ever sin.
So, can you tell me when my luck
is going to begin?

Ing

Today in school, in science class,
as we were all dissecting,
when all the kids would look away
their frogs I was collecting.
But soon enough the teacher
started doing some detecting.
She looked inside my frog-filled desk
and did her own inspecting.
She turned to me, and to the door
her finger was directing.
She sent me to the principal...
What were you expecting?

Sick and Tired

I'm tired of swinging.
I'm tired of singing.
I'm so sick and tired
of jingle bell ringing.
I'm tired of dogs.
I'm tired of cats.
I'm tired of beetles,
spiders, and bats.
I'm tired of girls.
I'm tired of boys.
I'm tired of playing
with all of my toys.
If I wasn't so tired,
I'd complain more instead,
but I'm so sick and tired
that I'm going to bed.

Little Moe

Teeny Tiny Little Moe.
Catch your father by his toe.
If he hollers, you will pay.
Do the dishes every day!

Traffic Light

Red, Yellow, and Green.
Oh, what do they mean?
Are they colors to guide us
or just there to be seen?
Red, Yellow, and Green.
What a marvelous team.
Never appear at the same time
but too often they're seen.

Pack of Lies

My sister used to lie a lot
but now she's honest, see.
And the sudden change in her
is all because of me.
Now she can never fib,
even if she tries
because I got inside her head
and stole her pack of lies.

Random Things

Triangles, circles,
rectangles, and squares.

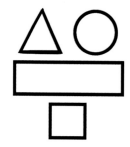

Apples and oranges,
peaches and pears.

Lions, tigers,
mosquitoes, and flies.

Cherries and lemons
and blueberry pies.

What Goes Around

What goes around
comes around
and comes around again.
But since I threw my boomerang
I haven't seen it in
seven days and seven nights.
I'm wondering if it's still in flight.
I'll search the world until I find...

...*BANG!*
Never mind.

Not My Birthday

I know it's not my birthday,
but I really have to say,
I really wouldn't mind
if you bought me gifts today.
It may sound kind of selfish,
but I'd thank you if you did.
So, go ahead, give me a break,
I'm just a little kid.

A Lot on My Mind

If I ignore you
or don't pay attention,
I guess right now
is a good time to mention,
that it's not your fault—
and if you look, you will find
that today I just have
a lot on my mind.

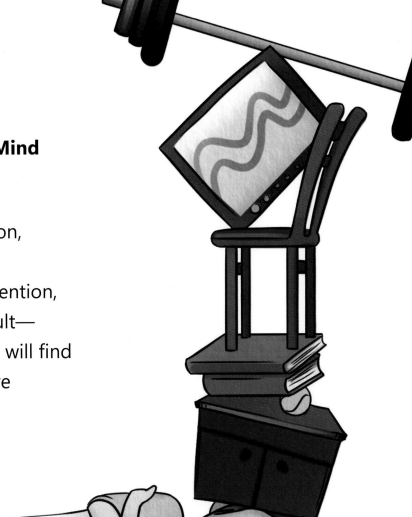

Allowance

Look Dad,
it's time to chat
about a little of this
and a little of that.
I've been watching what I eat,
and yesterday,
I walked an old lady across the street.
My grades are good,
and my room has stayed clean.
I filled the fireplace with wood
and I have not been mean.
What I'm trying to say
is that I'm improving my many talents.
So, Dad,
can I have a raise in my allowance?

Ice Cream Man

Ice cream, ice cream,
ice cream man!
Bring us some ice cream
as fast as you can.
Bring us vanilla
and chocolate—two dips.
Bring us some ice cream
that's cold on our lips.
Ice cream, ice cream,
ice cream man!
Bring us some ice cream
as fast as you can.

Just Because

Just because I like you,
just because you're there,
just because you show me
that you really care.
Just because you're with me,
just because we blend,
just because you'll always
be my favorite friend.